SNOW DAY SETS to KNIT

Hat & Mitten Sets for the WHOLE family!

Everybody bundle up! The days of snowmen and sledding are on their way, so why not get your family ready now? These toasty hats and matching mittens are excellent chill chasers, and they're sized for toddlers to adults. All seven sets and an extra pair of mittens use medium weight yarn—and these patterns are easy for anyone with intermediate knitting skills. We also include instructions to work on 2 or 4 needles. So let it snow! Your loved ones will romp and play on those wintry days while keeping cozy in your knitted creations.

To keep the wintry fun going indoors, too, see page 21 for a delicious hot cocoa recipe everyone will enjoy!

Table of Contents

A Visit with Lila Sargent

"I lived in Maine for years," says Lila Sargent. "I knitted all the time then. I mostly taught myself how to knit from a book and with a little help from friends and neighbors. When my grandson was born in 1990, I moved to Florida to be near him. I stopped knitting for a while.

"Then, a couple of years ago, I needed something to help me relax. I started knitting again —and filled up the house with sweaters! Eventually, I donated all those sweaters to charity and started designing hats and mittens."

Lila adds, "I like to knit while I watch my favorite baseball team. I'm glad the neighbors can't hear me yelling at the umpires!"

LEISURE ARTS, INC.
Little Rock, Arkansas

Basic Mittens

Size: Toddler{Child - Small Adult - Large Adult}

Palm Circumference (measured above thumb):
5½{6½-7½-9}" / 14{16.5-19-23} cm

Size Note: Instructions are written for Toddler size, with Child, Small Adult, and Large Adult sizes in braces { }. Instructions will be easier to read if you circle all the numbers pertaining to your size. If only one number is given, it applies to all sizes.

MATERIALS
Medium Weight Yarn 🧶 **MEDIUM 4**
　　[7 ounces, 364 yards
　　(198 grams, 333 meters) per skein]:
　　　1 skein
　or
　　[5 ounces, 244 yards
　　(141 grams, 223 meters) per skein]:
　　　1 skein
　and
　　Small amounts of contrasting colors for stripes
　Straight knitting needles for 2-Needle Mittens **or** double pointed needles (set of 4) for 4-Needle Mittens, sizes 6 (4 mm) **and** 8 (5 mm) **or** sizes needed for gauge
　Markers
　Scrap yarn or stitch holder
　Yarn needle

Techniques used: K2 tog *(Fig. 1, page 33)*, M1 *(Figs. 6a & b, page 34)*, M1P *(Figs. 7a & b, page 34)*, P2 tog *(Fig. 3, page 33)*

GAUGE: With larger size needles, in Stockinette Stitch, 18 sts and 24 rows/rnds = 4" (10 cm)

2-NEEDLE MITTEN (Make 2)
CUFF
With smaller size needles, cast on 26{30-34-42} sts.

Row 1: K3, P2, (K2, P2) across to last st, K1.

Row 2 (Right side): P1, K2, (P2, K2) across to last 3 sts, P3.

Loop a short piece of yarn through any stitch to mark Row 2 as **right** side.

Repeat Rows 1 and 2 until Cuff measures 2½{2¾-3-3}" / 6.5{7-7.5-7.5} cm increasing 1{1-2-0} st(s) evenly spaced on last row **and** ending by working a **wrong** side row *(see Zeros and Increasing Evenly Across a Row or Round, page 33)*: 27{31-36-42} sts.

HAND
Change to larger size needles.

Row 1 (Right side): K 13{15-17-20}, place marker for Thumb gusset *(see Markers, page 33)*, M1, K1{1-2-2}, M1, place marker for Thumb gusset, knit across: 29{33-38-44} sts.

Row 2: Purl to marker, slip marker, M1P, purl to marker, M1P, slip marker, purl across: 31{35-40-46} sts.

Row 3: Knit to marker, slip marker, M1, knit to marker, M1, slip marker, knit across: 33{37-42-48} sts.

Rows 4 thru 5{5-7-9}: Repeat Rows 2 and 3, 1{1-2-3} time(s): 37{41-50-60} sts [11{11-16-20} sts between Thumb markers].

Work even until Mitten measures approximately 4{4¾-5¼-5¾}" / 10{12-13.5-14.5} cm from cast on edge, ending by working a **purl** row.

Instructions continued on page 4

Basic Mittens

Instructions continued from page 2

PALM

Row 1: Knit to first Thumb marker, remove marker and place next 11{11-16-20} sts on scrap yarn or stitch holder, remove second marker, turn; add on 1{1-2-2} st(s), *(Figs. 5a & b, page 34)*, turn; knit across: 27{31-36-42} sts.

Work even until Mitten measures approximately 6{7-7¾-9¼}" / 15{18-19.5-23.5} cm from cast on edge, ending by working a **purl** row.

SHAPING

Row 1: (K2, K2 tog) across to last 3{3-4-2} sts, K 0{0-1-2}, (K2 tog, K1) 1{1-1-0} time: 20{23-27-32} sts.

Row 2: Purl across.

Row 3: K1{2-2-1}, K2 tog across to last st, K1: 11{13-15-17} sts.

Row 4: P2, P2 tog across to last st, P1: 7{8-9-10} sts.

Cut yarn leaving a long end. Thread yarn needle with end and weave through remaining sts, gathering tightly to close. With same end, weave seam *(Fig. 9, page 34)*.

THUMB

Row 1: Cast on 1{1-2-2} st(s); with **right** side facing, slip sts from scrap yarn or stitch holder onto empty larger size needle and knit across: 12{12-18-22} sts.

Row 2: Add on 1{1-2-2} st(s), purl across: 13{13-20-24} sts.

Work even until Thumb measures approximately 1½{2-2½-2¾}" / 4{5-6.5-7} cm, ending by working a **purl** row.

Next Row: K2{2-1-1}, K2 tog across to last st, K1: 8{8-11-13} sts.

Cut yarn. Thread yarn needle with end and weave through remaining sts, gathering tightly to close. With same end, weave seam.

4-NEEDLE MITTEN (Make 2)

CUFF

With smaller size needles, cast on 24{28-32-36} sts and distribute evenly on double pointed needles; place marker *(see Markers, page 33)*, join to work in rounds, being careful not to twist.

Work in K2, P2 ribbing around for 2½{2¾-3-3}" / 6.5{7-7.5-7.5} cm increasing 1{1-2-4} st(s) evenly spaced on last rnd *(see Increasing Evenly Across a Row or Round, page 33)*: 25{29-34-40} sts.

HAND

Change to larger size needles.

Rnd 1 (Right side): K 12{14-16-19}, place marker for Thumb gusset, M1, K1{1-2-2}, M1, place marker for Thumb gusset, knit around: 27{31-36-42} sts.

Rnds 2 thru 5{5-7-9}: Knit to marker, slip marker, M1, knit to marker, M1, slip marker, knit around: 35{39-48-58} sts [11{11-16-20} sts between Thumb markers].

Work even until Mitten measures approximately 4{4¾-5¼-5¾}" / 10{12-13.5-14.5} cm from cast on edge.

PALM

Rnd 1: Knit to first Thumb marker, remove marker and place next 11{11-16-20} sts on scrap yarn or stitch holder, remove second marker, turn; add on 1{1-2-2} st(s) *(Figs. 5a & b, page 34)*, turn; knit around: 25{29-34-40} sts.

Work even until Mitten measures approximately 6{7-7¾-9¼}" / 15{18-19.5-23.5] cm from cast on edge.

SHAPING

Rnd 1: (K2, K2 tog) around to last 1{1-2-0} st(s) *(see Zeros, page 33)*, K1{1-2-1}: 19{22-26-30} sts.

Rnd 2: Knit around.

Rnd 3: K1{0-0-0}, K2 tog around: 10{11-13-15} sts.

Rnd 4: K 0{1-1-1}, K2 tog around: 5{6-7-8} sts.

Cut yarn. Thread yarn needle with end and weave through remaining sts, gathering tightly to close.

THUMB

With **right** side facing, slip sts from scrap yarn or stitch holder onto double pointed needles; pick up 1{1-2-2} st(s) in added-on sts of Hand *(Fig. 8, page 34)*. Distribute sts evenly on needles: 12{12-18-22} sts.

Work even until Thumb measures approximately 1½{2-2½-2¾}" / 4{5-6.5-7} cm.

Next Row: K2 tog around: 6{6-9-11} sts.

Cut yarn. Thread yarn needle with end and weave through remaining sts, gathering tightly to close.

Shown on page 3

MITTENS

Work 2-Needle or 4-Needle Basic Mittens, pages 2-5, changing color as follows *(see Changing Colors in Ribbing, page 33)*:

Cast on with Lt Pink and work ¾{¾-1-1}" / 2{2-2.5-2.5} cm; change to Dk Pink and work ¾{¾-1-1}" / 2{2-2.5-2.5} cm; change to Lt Pink and complete Ribbing to specified length.

Work Hand with Lt Pink; work Palm with Dk Pink; then work Thumb with Lt Pink.

Winter in the Tropics Set

◐◼◼◻ INTERMEDIATE

Size: Toddler{Child - Small Adult - Large Adult}

Finished Hat Circumference: 16{16¾-18¾-20½}"
40.5{42.5-47.5-52} cm

Size Note: Instructions are written for Toddler size, with Child, Small Adult, and Large Adult sizes in braces { }. Instructions will be easier to read if you circle all the numbers pertaining to your size. If only one number is given, it applies to all sizes.

MATERIALS
Medium Weight Yarn (4 MEDIUM)
[5 ounces, 244 yards
(141 grams, 223 meters) per skein]:
1 skein
Straight knitting needles for 2-Needle Hat **or** double pointed needles (set of 4) for 4-Needle Hat, sizes 6 (4 mm) **and** 8 (5 mm) **or** sizes needed for gauge
Yarn needle

Techniques used: K2 tog *(Fig. 1, page 33)*

GAUGE: With larger size needles, in Stockinette Stitch, 18 sts and 24 rows/rnds = 4" (10 cm)

2-NEEDLE HAT
RIBBING
With smaller size needles, cast on 74{78-82-90} sts.

Row 1 (Right side): K4, P1, (K3, P1) across to last st, K1.

Loop a short piece of yarn through any stitch to mark Row 1 as **right** side.

Row 2: P1, K1, (P3, K1) across to last 4 sts, P4.

Repeat Rows 1 and 2 until Ribbing measures 1½" (4 cm), increasing 0{0-2-2} sts evenly spaced across last row **and** ending by working a **wrong** side row *(see Zeros and Increasing Evenly Across a Row or Round, page 33)*: 74{78-84-92} sts.

BODY
Change to larger size needles.

Row 1: K 11, (P 10, K 10) across to last 3{7-13-21} sts, P2{6-10-10}, K1{1-3-11}.

Row 2: P1{1-3-1}, K2{6-10-0}, (P 10, K 10) across to last 11 sts, P 11.

Row 3: K1, P1, K 10, (P 10, K 10) across to last 2{6-12-0} sts, P1{5-10-0}, K1{1-2-0}.

Row 4: P1{1-2-0}, K1{5-10-0}, P 10, (K 10, P 10) across to last 2 sts, K1, P1.

Row 5: K1, P2, K 10, (P 10, K 10) across to last 21{5-11-19} sts, P 10{4-10-10}, K 11{1-1-9}.

Row 6: P 11{1-1-9}, K 10{4-10-10}, P 10, (K 10, P 10) across to last 3 sts, K2, P1.

Row 7: K1, P3, K 10, (P 10, K 10) across to last 0{4-10-18} sts, P 0{3-9-10}, K 0{1-1-8}.

Row 8: P 0{1-1-8}, K 0{3-9-10}, P 10, (K 10, P 10) across to last 4 sts, K3, P1.

Row 9: K1, P4, (K 10, P 10) across to last 9{13-19-7} sts, K9{10-10-7}, P 0{2-8-0}, K 0{1-1-0}.

Row 10: P 0{1-1-0}, K 0{2-8-0}, P9{10-10-7}, (K 10, P 10) across to last 5 sts, K4, P1.

Instructions continued on page 8

Winter in the Tropics Set

Instructions continued from page 6

Row 11: K1, P5, (K 10, P 10) across to last 8{12-18-6} sts, K8{10-10-6}, P 0{1-7-0}, K 0{1-1-0}.

Row 12: P 0{1-1-0}, K 0{1-7-0}, P8{10-10-6}, (K 10, P 10) across to last 6 sts, K5, P1.

Row 13: K1, P6, (K 10, P 10) across to last 7{11-17-5} sts, K7{11-10-5}, P 0{0-6-0}, K 0{0-1-0}.

Row 14: P 0{0-1-0}, K 0{0-6-0}, P7{11-10-5}, (K 10, P 10) across to last 7 sts, K6, P1.

Row 15: K1, P7, (K 10, P 10) across to last 6{10-16-4} sts, K6{10-10-4}, P 0{0-5-0}, K 0{0-1-0}.

Row 16: P 0{0-1-0}, K 0{0-5-0}, P6{10-10-4}, (K 10, P 10) across to last 8 sts, K7, P1.

Row 17: K1, P8, (K 10, P 10) across to last 5{9-15-3} sts, K5{9-10-3}, P 0{0-4-0}, K 0{0-1-0}.

Row 18: P 0{0-1-0}, K 0{0-4-0}, P5{9-10-3}, (K 10, P 10) across to last 9 sts, K8, P1.

Row 19: K1, P9, (K 10, P 10) across to last 4{8-14-2} sts, K4{8-10-2}, P 0{0-3-0}, K 0{0-1-0}.

Row 20: P 0{0-1-0}, K 0{0-3-0}, P4{8-10-2}, (K 10, P 10) across to last 10 sts, K9, P1.

Row 21: K1, P 10, (K 10, P 10) across to last 3{7-13-1} st(s), K3{7-10-1}, P 0{0-2-0}, K 0{0-1-0}.

Row 22: P 0{0-1-0}, K 0{0-2-0}, P3{7-10-1}, K 10, (P 10, K 10) across to last, P1.

Row 23: K2, P 10, (K 10, P 10) across to last 2{6-12-20} sts, K2{6-10-10}, P 0{0-1-9}, K 0{0-1-1}.

Row 24: P 0{0-1-1}, K 0{0-1-9}, P2{6-10-10}, K 10, (P 10, K 10) across to last 2 sts, P2.

Sizes Child, Small Adult, and Large Adult Only
Next {6-10-14} Rows: Continue in pattern, moving spiral one stitch to the left every **right** side row by working one additional purl stitch following the knit edge stitch.

CROWN SHAPING - All sizes

Row 1: K5{3-3-5}, K2 tog, (K4, K2 tog) across to last st, K1: 62{65-70-77} sts.

Row 2: Purl across.

Row 3: K4{2-2-4}, K2 tog, (K3, K2 tog) across to last st, K1: 50{52-56-62} sts.

Row 4: Purl across.

Row 5: K3{1-1-3}, K2 tog, (K2, K2 tog) across to last st, K1: 38{39-42-47} sts.

Row 6: Purl across.

Row 7: (K1, K2 tog) across to last 2{3-3-2} sts, K2{3-3-2}: 26{27-29-32} sts.

Row 8: Purl across.

Row 9: K1, K2 tog across to last 1{2-2-1} st(s), K1{2-2-1}: 14{15-16-17} sts.

Cut yarn leaving a long end. Thread yarn needle with end and weave through remaining sts, gathering tightly to close. With same end, weave seam *(Fig. 9, page 34)*.

4-NEEDLE HAT
RIBBING

With smaller size needles, cast on 72{76-80-88} sts and distribute evenly on double pointed needles; place marker *(see Markers, page 33)*, join to work in rounds, being careful not to twist.

Rnd 1 (Right side): (K3, P1) around.

Repeat Rnd 1 until Ribbing measures 1½" (4 cm), increasing 0{0-2-2} sts evenly spaced on last rnd *(see Zeros and Increasing Evenly Across a Row or Round, page 33)*: 72{76-82-90} sts.

BODY
Change to larger size needles.

Rnds 1 and 2: P 10, (K 10, P 10) around to last 2{6-12-0} sts, K2{6-10-0}, P 0{0-2-0}.

Rnds 3 and 4: K1, P 10, (K 10, P 10) around to last 1{5-11-19} st(s), K1{5-10-10}, P 0{0-1-9}.

Rnds 5 and 6: K2, P 10, (K 10, P 10) around to last 0{4-10-18} sts, K 0{4-10-10}, P 0{0-0-8}.

Rnds 7 and 8: K3, P 10, (K 10, P 10) around to last 19{3-9-17} sts, K 10{3-9-10}, P9{0-0-7}.

Rnds 9 and 10: K4, P 10, (K 10, P 10) around to last 18{2-8-16} sts, K 10{2-8-10}, P8{0-0-6}.

Rnds 11 and 12: K5, P 10, (K 10, P 10) around to last 17{1-7-15} st(s), K 10{1-7-10}, P7{0-0-5}.

Rnds 13 and 14: K6, P 10, (K 10, P 10) around to last 16{0-6-14} sts, K 10{0-6-10}, P6{0-0-4}.

Rnds 15 and 16: K7, P 10, (K 10, P 10) around to last 15{19-5-13} sts, K 10{10-5-10}, P5{9-0-3}.

Rnds 17 and 18: K8, P 10, (K 10, P 10) around to last 14{18-4-12} sts, K 10{10-4-10}, P4{8-0-2}.

Rnds 19 and 20: K9, P 10, (K 10, P 10) around to last 13{17-3-11} sts, K 10{10-3-10}, P3{7-0-1}.

Rnds 21 and 22: (K 10, P 10) around to last 12{16-2-10} sts, K 10{10-2-10}, P2{6-0-0}.

Rnds 23 and 24: P1, K 10, (P 10, K 10) around to last 1{5-11-19} st(s), P1{5-0-10}, K 0{0-1-9}.

**Sizes Child, Small Adult, and Large Adult Only
Next {6-10-14} Rnds:** Continue in pattern, moving spiral one stitch to the left, every two rounds, by beginning round with one additional purl stitch.

CROWN SHAPING - All sizes
Rnd 1: K4{2-2-4}, K2 tog, (K4, K2 tog) around: 60{63-68-75} sts.

Rnd 2: Knit around.

Rnd 3: K3{1-1-3}, K2 tog, (K3, K2 tog) around: 48{50-54-60} sts.

Rnd 4: Knit around.

Rnd 5: K2{0-0-2}, K2 tog, (K2, K2 tog) around: 36{37-40-45} sts.

Rnd 6: Knit around.

Rnd 7: (K1, K2 tog) around to last 0{1-1-0} st, K 0{1-1-0}: 24{25-27-30} sts.

Rnd 8: Knit around.

Rnd 9: K2 tog around to last 0{1-1-0} st, K 0{1-1-0}: 12{13-14-15} sts.

Cut yarn. Thread yarn needle with end and weave through remaining sts, gathering tightly to close.

MITTENS
Work 2-Needle or 4-Needle Basic Mittens, pages 2-5.

Winter Sunshine Set

Size: Toddler{Child - Small Adult - Large Adult}

Finished Hat Circumference: 16{16¾-18¾-20½}"
40.5{42.5-47.5-52} cm

Size Note: Instructions are written for Toddler size, with Child, Small Adult, and Large Adult sizes in braces { }. Instructions will be easier to read if you circle all the numbers pertaining to your size. If only one number is given, it applies to all sizes.

MATERIALS

Medium Weight Yarn 🧶 **4**
[7 ounces, 364 yards
(198 grams, 333 meters) per skein]:
Yellow - 1 skein
Lt Blue - small amount
Straight knitting needles for 2-Needle Hat **or**
double pointed needles (set of 4) for 4-Needle
Hat, sizes 6 (4 mm) **and** 8 (5 mm) **or** sizes
needed for gauge
Yarn needle

Techniques used: K2 tog (*Fig. 1, page 33*)

GAUGE: With larger size needles, in Stockinette Stitch,
18 sts and 24 rows/rnds = 4" (10 cm)

When instructed to slip a stitch, always slip as if to knit.

2-NEEDLE HAT
RIBBING

With Yellow and smaller size needles, cast on
74{78-82-90} sts.

Row 1: P2, (K2, P2) across.

Row 2 (Right side): K2, (P2, K2) across.

Loop a short piece of yarn through any stitch to mark
Row 2 as **right** side.

Repeat Rows 1 and 2 for 1½" (4 cm), increasing 0{0-2-2} sts
evenly spaced across last row **and** ending by working a
wrong side row (*see Zeros and Increasing Evenly Across
a Row or Round, page 33*): 74{78-84-92} sts.

BODY
Change to larger size needles.

Row 1: K4{4-2-2}, slip 1, (K3, slip 1) across to last st, K1.

Row 2: Purl across.

Repeat Rows 1 and 2 for pattern until Hat measures
approximately 3¼{3¾-4-4½}" / 8{9.5-10-11.5} cm from
cast on edge, ending by working a **right** side row.

Next 4{4-6-6} Rows: With Lt Blue, repeat Row 2 once,
then repeat Rows 1 and 2, 1{1-2-2} time(s); then repeat
Row 1 once **more**; at end of last row, cut Lt Blue.

With Yellow and beginning with Row 2, work in pattern
until Hat measures approximately 5½{6½-7¼-8}" /
14{16.5-18.5-20.5} cm from cast on edge, ending by
working a **purl** row.

CROWN SHAPING
Row 1: K5{3-3-5}, K2 tog, (K4, K2 tog) across to last st,
K1: 62{65-70-77} sts.

Row 2: Purl across.

Row 3: K4{2-2-4}, K2 tog, (K3, K2 tog) across to last st,
K1: 50{52-56-62} sts.

Instructions continued on page 30

Snow Drift Set

□■■■□ INTERMEDIATE

Size: Toddler{Child - Small Adult - Large Adult}

Finished Hat Circumference: 16{16¾-18¾-20½}"
40.5{42.5-47.5-52} cm

Size Note: Instructions are written for Toddler size, with Child, Small Adult, and Large Adult sizes in braces { }. Instructions will be easier to read if you circle all the numbers pertaining to your size. If only one number is given, it applies to all sizes.

MATERIALS
Medium Weight Yarn (4)
   [7 ounces, 364 yards
   (198 grams, 333 meters) per skein]:
   White - 1 skein
   Tan - small amount
Straight knitting needles for 2-Needle Hat **or**
   double pointed needles (set of 4) for 4-Needle
   Hat, sizes 6 (4 mm) **and** 8 (5 mm) **or** sizes
   needed for gauge
Yarn needle

Techniques used: K2 tog *(Fig. 1, page 33)*

GAUGE: With larger size needles, in Stockinette Stitch,
   18 sts and 24 rows/rnds = 4" (10 cm)

When instructed to slip a stitch, always slip as if to **knit** unless instructed otherwise.

2-NEEDLE HAT
RIBBING
With White and smaller size needles, cast on 74{78-82-90} sts.

Row 1 (Right side): (K1, P3) across to last 2 sts, K2.

Loop a short piece of yarn through any stitch to mark Row 1 as **right** side.

Row 2: P2, (K3, P1) across.

Rows 3 and 4: Repeat Rows 1 and 2.

Row 5: With Tan, knit across *(see Changing Colors in Ribbing, page 33)*.

Row 6: P2, (K3, P1) across.

Rows 7 and 8: Repeat Rows 1 and 2, increasing 0{0-2-2} sts evenly spaced across last row *(see Zeros and Increasing Evenly Across a Row or Round, page 33)*: 74{78-84-92} sts.

Cut Tan.

BODY
Change to larger size needles.

Row 1: With White, K3{1-1-3}, slip 1, (K2, slip 1) across to last st, K1.

Row 2: Purl across.

Repeat Rows 1 and 2 for pattern until Hat measures approximately 5½{6½-7¼-8}" / 14{16.5-18.5-20.5} cm from cast on edge, ending by working a **purl** row.

CROWN SHAPING
Row 1: K5{3-3-5}, K2 tog, (K4, K2 tog) across to last st, K1: 62{65-70-77} sts.

Row 2: Purl across.

Row 3: K4{2-2-4}, K2 tog, (K3, K2 tog) across to last st, K1: 50{52-56-62} sts.

Instructions continued on page 31

Red Berries Set

Size: Toddler{Child - Small Adult - Large Adult}

Finished Hat Circumference: 16{16¾-18¾-20½}"
40.5{42.5-47.5-52} cm

Size Note: Instructions are written for Toddler size, with Child, Small Adult, and Large Adult sizes in braces { }. Instructions will be easier to read if you circle all the numbers pertaining to your size. If only one number is given, it applies to all sizes.

MATERIALS
Medium Weight Yarn **[MEDIUM 4]**
[7 ounces, 364 yards
(198 grams, 333 meters) per skein]:
Red - 1 skein
Blue - small amount
Straight knitting needles for 2-Needle Hat **or** double pointed needles (set of 4) for 4-Needle Hat, sizes 6 (4 mm) **and** 8 (5 mm) **or** sizes needed for gauge
Yarn needle

Techniques used: K2 tog *(Fig. 1, page 33),* K3 tog *(Fig. 2, page 33),* P3 tog *(Fig. 4, page 34)*

GAUGE: With larger size needles, in Stockinette Stitch, 18 sts and 24 rows/rnds = 4" (10 cm)

2-NEEDLE HAT
RIBBING
With Red and smaller size needles, cast on 74{78-86-90} sts.

Row 1: P1, K2, (P2, K2) across to last 3 sts, P3.

Row 2 (Right side): K3, P2, (K2, P2) across to last st, K1.

Loop a short piece of yarn through any stitch to mark Row 2 as **right** side.

Rows 3-7: Repeat Rows 1 and 2 twice, then repeat Row 1 once **more**.

Row 8: With Blue, knit across; cut Blue *(see Changing Colors in Ribbing, page 33).*

Row 9: With Red, purl across.

Row 10: K3, P2, (K2, P2) across to last st, K1.

Rows 11-13: Repeat Rows 1 and 2 once, then repeat Row 1 once **more**.

BODY
Change to larger size needles.

Row 1: Purl across.

Row 2: K1, ★ (K, P, K) **all** in next st, P3 tog; repeat from ★ across to last st, K1.

Row 3: Purl across.

Row 4: K1, ★ P3 tog, (K, P, K) **all** in next st; repeat from ★ across to last st, K1.

Repeat Rows 1-4, 1{1-2-2} time(s).

Instructions continued on page 16

Red Berries Set

Instructions continued from page 14

CROWN RIBBING
Row 1: K1, P2, (K2, P2) across to last 3 sts, K3.

Row 2: P3, K2, (P2, K2) across to last st, P1.

Rows 3 and 4: Repeat Rows 1 and 2.

Row 5: With Blue, knit across; cut Blue.

Row 6: With Red, purl across.

Repeat Rows 1 and 2 until Hat measures approximately 5½{6½-7¼-8}" / 14{16.5-18.5-20.5} cm from cast on edge, ending by working a **wrong** side row.

Cut Red.

CROWN SHAPING
Row 1: With Blue, K5{3-5-3}, K2 tog, (K4, K2 tog) across to last st, K1: 62{65-72-75} sts.

Row 2: Purl across.

Row 3: K4{2-4-2}, K2 tog, (K3, K2 tog) across to last st, K1: 50{52-58-60} sts.

Row 4: Purl across.

Row 5: K3{1-3-1}, K2 tog, (K2, K2 tog) across to last st, K1: 38{39-44-45} sts.

Row 6: Purl across.

Row 7: (K1, K2 tog) across to last 2{3-2-3} sts, K2{3-2-3}: 26{27-30-31} sts.

Row 8: Purl across.

Row 9: K1, K2 tog across to last 1{2-1-2} st(s), K1{2-1-2}: 14{15-16-17} sts.

Cut yarn leaving a long end. Thread yarn needle with end and weave through remaining sts, gathering tightly to close. With same end, weave seam *(Fig. 9, page 34)*.

4-NEEDLE HAT
RIBBING
With Red and smaller size needles, cast on 72{76-84-88} sts and distribute evenly on double pointed needles; place marker *(see Markers, page 33)*, join to work in rounds, being careful not to twist.

Rnds 1-7: (K2, P2) around.

Rnd 8: With Blue, knit around; cut Blue *(see Changing Colors in Ribbing, page 33)*.

Rnd 9: With Red, knit around.

Rnds 10-13: (K2, P2) around.

BODY

Change to larger size needles.

Rnd 1: With Red, purl around.

Rnd 2: ★ (P, K, P) **all** in next st, K3 tog; repeat from ★ around.

Rnd 3: Purl around.

Rnd 4: ★ K3 tog, (P, K, P) **all** in next st; repeat from ★ around.

Repeat Rows 1-4, 1{1-2-2} time(s).

CROWN RIBBING

Rnds 1-4: (P2, K2) around.

Rnd 5: With Blue, knit around; cut Blue.

Rnd 6: With Red, knit around.

Work in P2, K2 ribbing until Hat measures approximately 5½{6½-7¼-8}" / 14{16.5-18.5-20.5} cm from cast on edge.

Cut Red.

CROWN SHAPING

Rnd 1: With Blue, K4{2-4-2}, K2 tog, (K4, K2 tog) around: 60{63-70-73} sts.

Rnd 2: Knit around.

Rnd 3: K3{1-3-1}, K2 tog, (K3, K2 tog) around: 48{50-56-58} sts.

Rnd 4: Knit around.

Rnd 5: K2{0-2-0} *(see Zeros, page 33)*, K2 tog, (K2, K2 tog) around: 36{37-42-43} sts.

Rnd 6: Knit around.

Rnd 7: (K1, K2 tog) around to last 0{1-0-1} st, K 0{1-0-1}: 24{25-28-29} sts.

Rnd 8: Knit around.

Rnd 9: K2 tog around to last 0{1-0-1} st, K 0{1-0-1}: 12{13-14-15} sts.

Cut yarn. Thread yarn needle with end and weave through remaining sts, gathering tightly to close.

MITTENS

Work 2-Needle or 4-Needle Basic Mittens, pages 2-5, changing color in ribbing as follows:

Cast on with Red and work 1½{1¾-2-2}" / 4{4.5-5-5} cm; change to Blue *(see Changing Colors in Ribbing, page 33)* and work 1" (2.5 cm). Cut Blue; with Red complete Mitten.

Blue Ice Set

⬤■■□ INTERMEDIATE

Size: Toddler{Child - Small Adult - Large Adult}

Finished Hat Circumference: 16{16¾-18¾-20½}"
40.5{42.5-47.5-52} cm

Size Note: Instructions are written for Toddler size, with Child, Small Adult, and Large Adult sizes in braces { }. Instructions will be easier to read if you circle all the numbers pertaining to your size. If only one number is given, it applies to all sizes.

MATERIALS
Medium Weight Yarn **④ MEDIUM**
[7 ounces, 364 yards
(198 grams, 333 meters) per skein]:
Lt Blue - 1 skein
Blue - small amount
Straight knitting needles for 2-Needle Hat **or**
double pointed needles (set of 4) for 4-Needle
Hat, sizes 6 (4 mm) **and** 8 (5 mm) **or** sizes
needed for gauge
Yarn needle

Techniques used: K2 tog (*Fig. 1, page 33*)

GAUGE: With larger size needles, in Stockinette Stitch, 18 sts and 24 rows/rnds = 4" (10 cm)

2-NEEDLE HAT
RIBBING
With Lt Blue and smaller size needles, cast on 74{78-86-90} sts.

Row 1: P1, K2, (P2, K2) across to last 3 sts, P3.

Row 2 (Right side): K3, P2, (K2, P2) across to last st, K1.

Loop a short piece of yarn through any stitch to mark Row 2 as **right** side.

Repeat Rows 1 and 2 for 1½" (4 cm), increasing 0{2-0-2} sts evenly spaced across last row **and** ending by working a **wrong** side row (*see Zeros and Increasing Evenly Across a Row or Round, page 33*): 74{80-86-92} sts.

BODY
Change to larger size needles.

Row 1: K6, P1, (K5, P1) across to last st, K1.

Row 2: P1, K1, (P5, K1) across to last 6 sts, P6.

Row 3: K1, P1, (K5, P1) across to last 6 sts, K6.

Row 4: P6, K1, (P5, K1) across to last st, P1.

Row 5: K2, (P1, K5) across.

Row 6: (P5, K1) across to last 2 sts, P2.

Row 7: K3, P1, (K5, P1) across to last 4 sts, K4.

Row 8: P4, K1, (P5, K1) across to last 3 sts, P3.

Row 9: K4, P1, (K5, P1) across to last 3 sts, K3.

Row 10: P3, K1, (P5, K1) across to last 4 sts, P4.

Row 11: (K5, P1) across to last 2 sts, K2.

Row 12: P2, (K1, P5) across.

Rows 13 and 14: Repeat Rows 9 and 10.

Instructions continued on page 20

Blue Ice Set

Instructions continued from page 18

Toddler Size Only
Cut Lt Blue and continue with Blue.

All Sizes
Rows 15 and 16: Repeat Rows 7 and 8.

Rows 17 and 18: Repeat Rows 5 and 6.

Rows 19 and 20: Repeat Rows 3 and 4.

Child Size Only
Cut Lt Blue and continue with Blue.

All Sizes
Rows 21-24: Repeat Rows 1-4.

Small Adult Size Only
Cut Lt Blue and continue with Blue.

Sizes Child, Adult Small, and Adult Large Only
Repeat Rows 5-8.

Large Adult Size Only
Cut Lt Blue and continue with Blue.

Sizes Child, Adult Small, and Adult Large Only
Repeat Rows 9 thru {10-14-18}.

CROWN SHAPING - All sizes
Row 1: K5, K2 tog, (K4, K2 tog) across to last st, K1: 62{67-72-77} sts.

Row 2: Purl across; cut Blue.

Row 3: With Lt Blue, K4, K2 tog, (K3, K2 tog) across to last st, K1: 50{54-58-62} sts.

Row 4: Purl across.

Row 5: K3, K2 tog, (K2, K2 tog) across to last st, K1: 38{41-44-47} sts.

Row 6: Purl across.

Row 7: K2, K2 tog, (K1, K2 tog) across to last st, K1: 26{28-30-32} sts.

Row 8: Purl across.

Row 9: K1, K2 tog across to last st, K1: 14{15-16-17} sts.

Cut yarn leaving a long end. Thread yarn needle with end and weave through remaining sts, gathering tightly to close. With same end, weave seam *(Fig. 9, page 34)*.

4-NEEDLE HAT
RIBBING
With Lt Blue and smaller size needles, cast on 72{76-84-88} sts and distribute evenly on double pointed needles; place marker *(see Markers, page 33)*, join to work in rounds, being careful not to twist.

Work in K2, P2 ribbing around for 1½" (4 cm) increasing 0{2-0-2} sts evenly spaced on last rnd *(see Zeros and Increasing Evenly Across a Row or Round, page 33)*: 72{78-84-90} sts.

BODY
Change to larger size needles.

Rnds 1 and 2: (K5, P1) around.

Rnds 3 and 4: (P1, K5) around.

Rnds 5 and 6: K1, P1, (K5, P1) around to last 4 sts, K4.

Rnds 7 and 8: K2, P1, (K5, P1) around to last 3 sts, K3.

Rnds 9 and 10: K3, P1, (K5, P1) around to last 2 sts, K2.

Rnds 11 and 12: K4, P1, (K5, P1) around to last st, K1.

Rnds 13 and 14: Repeat Rnds 9 and 10.

Toddler Size Only
Cut Lt Blue and continue with Blue.

All Sizes
Rnds 15 and 16: Repeat Rnds 7 and 8.

Rnds 17 and 18: Repeat Rnds 5 and 6.

Rnds 19 and 20: Repeat Rnds 3 and 4.

Child Size Only
Cut Lt Blue and continue with Blue.

All Sizes
Rnds 21-24: Repeat Rnds 1-4.

Small Adult Size Only
Cut Lt Blue and continue with Blue.

Sizes Child, Adult Small, and Adult Large Only
Repeat Rnds 5-8.

Large Adult Size Only
Cut Lt Blue and continue with Blue.

Sizes Child, Adult Small, and Adult Large Only
Repeat Rnds 9 thru {10-14-18}.

CROWN SHAPING - All sizes
Rnd 1: (K4, K2 tog) around: 60{65-70-75} sts.

Rnd 2: Knit around; cut Blue.

Rnd 3: With Lt Blue, (K3, K2 tog) around: 48{52-56-60} sts.

Rnd 4: Knit around.

Rnd 5: (K2, K2 tog) around: 36{39-42-45} sts.

Rnd 6: Knit around.

Rnd 7: (K1, K2 tog) around: 24{26-28-30} sts.

Rnd 8: Knit around.

Rnd 9: K2 tog around: 12{13-14-15} sts.

Cut yarn. Thread yarn needle with end and weave through remaining sts, gathering tightly to close.

MITTENS
Work 2-Needle or 4-Needle Basic Mittens, pages 2-5, changing color in ribbing as follows *(see Changing Colors in Ribbing, page 33)*:

Cast on with Lt Blue and work 1½{1¾-2-2}" / 4{4.5-5-5} cm; change to Blue and work 1" (2.5 cm). Cut Blue; with Lt Blue complete Mitten.

Spicy Cocoa Mix

3½	cups firmly packed brown sugar
2	cups unsweetened cocoa
2	teaspoons ground cinnamon
½	teaspoon ground nutmeg
½	teaspoon ground cloves
¼	teaspoon salt

Process brown sugar, cocoa, cinnamon, nutmeg, cloves, and salt in a food processor until well blended. Store in an airtight container. Makes about 5 cups of cocoa mix. To serve, pour 6 ounces of hot milk over 1½ tablespoons of cocoa mix; stir until well blended. Top with miniature marshmallows.

Red Raspberry Set

Size: Child{Small Adult - Large Adult}

Finished Hat Circumference: 16½{19¼-22}"
42{49-56} cm

Size Note: Instructions are written for Child size, with Small Adult, and Large Adult sizes in braces { }. Instructions will be easier to read if you circle all the numbers pertaining to your size. If only one number is given, it applies to all sizes.

MATERIALS

Medium Weight Yarn
[5 ounces, 244 yards
(141 grams, 223 meters) per skein]: 1 skein
Straight knitting needles for 2-Needle Hat **or**
double pointed needles (set of 4) for 4-Needle
Hat, sizes 6 (4 mm) **and** 8 (5 mm) **or** sizes
needed for gauge
Cable needle
Yarn needle

Techniques used: K2 tog *(Fig. 1, page 33)*

GAUGE: With larger size needles, in Stockinette Stitch,
18 sts and 24 rows/rnds = 4" (10 cm)
With larger size needles, in pattern,
1 repeat (14 sts) = 2¾" wide (7 cm)

STITCH GUIDE

BACK CABLE (uses next 4 sts)
Slip next 2 sts onto cable needle and hold in **back** of work, K2 from left needle, K2 from cable needle.
FRONT CABLE (uses next 4 sts)
Slip next 2 sts onto cable needle and hold in **front** of work, K2 from left needle, K2 from cable needle.

2-NEEDLE HAT
RIBBING
With smaller size needles, cast on 74{86-98} sts.

Row 1: P1, K2, (P2, K2) across to last 3 sts, P3.

Row 2 (Right side): K3, P2, (K2, P2) across to last st, K1.

Loop a short piece of yarn through any stitch to mark Row 2 as **right** side.

Repeat Rows 1 and 2 for 1½" (4 cm), increasing 12{14-16} sts evenly spaced across last row **and** ending by working a **wrong** side row *(see Increasing Evenly Across a Row or Round, page 33)*: 86{100-114} sts.

BODY
Change to larger size needles.

Row 1: K1, P1, work Back Cable, work Front Cable, ★ (P1, work Back Cable) twice, work Front Cable; repeat from ★ across to last 6 sts, P1, work Back Cable, K1.

Row 2: P5, K1, P8, K1, ★ P4, K1, P8, K1; repeat from ★ across to last st, P1.

Instructions continued on page 24

Red Raspberry Set

Instructions continued from page 22

Row 3: K1, P1, K8, P1, ★ K4, P1, K8, P1; repeat from ★ across to last 5 sts, K5.

Row 4: P5, K1, P8, K1, ★ P4, K1, P8, K1; repeat from ★ across to last st, P1.

Repeat Rows 1-4 for pattern until Hat measures approximately 6½{7¼-8}" / 16.5{18.5-20.5} cm from cast on edge, ending by working a **wrong** side row.

CROWN SHAPING
Row 1: K6, K2 tog, (K5, K2 tog) across to last st, K1: 74{86-98} sts.

Row 2: Purl across.

Row 3: K5, K2 tog, (K4, K2 tog) across to last st, K1: 62{72-82} sts.

Row 4: Purl across.

Row 5: K4, K2 tog, (K3, K2 tog) across to last st, K1: 50{58-66} sts.

Row 6: Purl across.

Row 7: K3, K2 tog, (K2, K2 tog) across to last st, K1: 38{44-50} sts.

Row 8: Purl across.

Row 9: K2, K2 tog (K1, K2 tog) across to last st, K1: 26{30-34} sts.

Row 10: Purl across.

Row 11: K1, K2 tog across to last st, K1: 14{16-18} sts.

Cut yarn leaving a long end. Thread yarn needle with end and weave through remaining sts, gathering tightly to close. With same end, weave seam *(Fig. 9, page 34)*.

4-NEEDLE HAT
RIBBING
With smaller size needles, cast on 72{84-96} sts and distribute evenly on double pointed needles; place marker *(see Markers, page 33)*, join to work in rounds, being careful not to twist.

Work in K2, P2 ribbing around for 1½" (4 cm) increasing 12{14-16} sts evenly spaced on last rnd *(see Increasing Evenly Across a Row or Round, page 33)*: 84{98-112} sts.

BODY
Change to larger size needles.

Rnd 1: ★ (P1, work Back Cable) twice, work Front Cable; repeat from ★ around.

Rnds 2-4: ★ P1, K4, P1, K8; repeat from ★ around.

Repeat Rnds 1-4 for pattern until Hat measures approximately 6½{7¼-8}" / 16.5{18.5-20.5} cm from cast on edge.

CROWN SHAPING
Rnd 1: (K5, K2 tog) around: 72{84-96} sts.

Rnd 2: Knit around.

Row 3: (K4, K2 tog) around: 60{70-80} sts.

Rnd 4: Knit around.

Row 5: (K3, K2 tog) around: 48{56-64} sts.

Rnd 6: Knit around.

Row 7: (K2, K2 tog) around: 36{42-48} sts.

Rnd 8: Knit around.

Row 9: (K1, K2 tog) around: 24{28-32} sts.

Rnd 10: Knit around.

Row 11: K2 tog around: 12{14-16} sts.

Cut yarn. Thread yarn needle with end and weave through remaining sts, gathering tightly to close.

MITTENS
Work 2-Needle or 4-Needle Basic Mittens, pages 2-5.

Evergreen Set

Size: Toddler{Child - Small Adult - Large Adult}

Finished Hat Circumference: 16{16¾-18¾-20½}"
40.5{42.5-47.5-52} cm

Size Note: Instructions are written for Toddler size, with Child, Small Adult, and Large Adult sizes in braces { }. Instructions will be easier to read if you circle all the numbers pertaining to your size. If only one number is given, it applies to all sizes.

MATERIALS
Medium Weight Yarn [MEDIUM 4]
  [3 ounces, 146 yards
  (85 grams, 134 meters) per skein]:
  Variegated - 2 skeins
  Green - 1 skein
Straight knitting needles for 2-Needle Hat **or**
  double pointed needles (set of 4) for 4-Needle
  Hat, sizes 6 (4 mm) **and** 8 (5 mm) **or** sizes
  needed for gauge
Yarn needle

Techniques used: K2 tog *(Fig. 1, page 33)*, P2 tog *(Fig. 3, page 33)*

GAUGE: With larger size needles, in Stockinette Stitch, 18 sts and 24 rows/rnds = 4" / 10 cm

2-NEEDLE HAT
RIBBING
With Variegated and smaller size needles, cast on 74{78-82-90} sts.

Row 1 (Right side): K2, (P2, K2) across.

Loop a short piece of yarn through any stitch to mark Row 1 as **right** side.

Row 2: P2, (K2, P2) across.

Repeat Rows 1 and 2 until Ribbing measures 1½" (4 cm), increasing 0{0-2-2} sts evenly spaced across last row **and** ending by working a **wrong** side row *(see Zeros and Increasing Evenly Across a Row or Round, page 33)*: 74{78-84-92} sts.

BODY
Change to larger size needles.

Row 1: K 11, (P 10, K 10) across to last 3{7-13-21} sts, P2{6-10-10}, K1{1-3-11}.

Row 2: P1{1-3-1}, K2{6-10-0}, (P 10, K 10) across to last 11 sts, P 11.

Row 3: K1, P1, K 10, (P 10, K 10) across to last 2{6-12-0} sts, P1{5-10-0}, K1{1-2-0}.

Row 4: P1{1-2-0}, K1{5-10-0}, P 10, (K 10, P 10) across to last 2 sts, K1, P1.

Row 5: K1, P2, K 10, (P 10, K 10) across to last 21{5-11-19} sts, P 10{4-10-10}, K 11{1-1-9}.

Row 6: P 11{1-1-9}, K 10{4-10-10}, P 10, (K 10, P 10) across to last 3 sts, K2, P1.

Row 7: K1, P3, K 10, (P 10, K 10) across to last 0{4-10-18} sts, P 0{3-9-10}, K 0{1-1-8}.

Row 8: P 0{1-1-8}, K 0{3-9-10}, P 10, (K 10, P 10) across to last 4 sts, K3, P1.

Instructions continued on page 28

Evergreen Set

Instructions continued from page 26

Row 9: K1, P4, (K 10, P 10) across to last 9{13-19-7} sts, K9{10-10-7}, P 0{2-8-0}, K 0{1-1-0}.

Row 10: P 0{1-1-0}, K 0{2-8-0}, P9{10-10-7}, (K 10, P 10) across to last 5 sts, K4, P1.

Row 11: K1, P5, (K 10, P 10) across to last 8{12-18-6} sts, K8{10-10-6}, P 0{1-7-0}, K 0{1-1-0}.

Row 12: P 0{1-1-0}, K 0{1-7-0}, P8{10-10-6}, (K 10, P 10) across to last 6 sts, K5, P1.

Row 13: K1, P6, (K 10, P 10) across to last 7{11-17-5} sts, K7{11-10-5}, P 0{0-6-0}, K 0{0-1-0}.

Row 14: P 0{0-1-0}, K 0{0-6-0}, P7{11-10-5}, (K 10, P 10) across to last 7 sts, K6, P1.

Row 15: K1, P7, (K 10, P 10) across to last 6{10-16-4} sts, K6{10-10-4}, P 0{0-5-0}, K 0{0-1-0}.

Row 16: P 0{0-1-0}, K 0{0-5-0}, P6{10-10-4}, (K 10, P 10) across to last 8 sts, K7, P1.

Row 17: K1, P8, (K 10, P 10) across to last 5{9-15-3} sts, K5{9-10-3}, P 0{0-4-0}, K 0{0-1-0}.

Row 18: P 0{0-1-0}, K 0{0-4-0}, P5{9-10-3}, (K 10, P 10) across to last 9 sts, K8, P1.

Row 19: K1, P9, (K 10, P 10) across to last 4{8-14-2} sts, K4{8-10-2}, P 0{0-3-0}, K 0{0-1-0}.

Row 20: P 0{0-1-0}, K 0{0-3-0}, P4{8-10-2}, (K 10, P 10) across to last 10 sts, K9, P1.

Row 21: K1, P 10, (K 10, P 10) across to last 3{7-13-1} st(s), K3{7-10-1}, P 0{0-2-0}, K 0{0-1-0}.

Row 22: P 0{0-1-0}, K 0{0-2-0}, P3{7-10-1}, K 10, (P 10, K 10) across to last, P1.

Row 23: K2, P 10, (K 10, P 10) across to last 2{6-12-20} sts, K2{6-10-10}, P 0{0-1-9}, K 0{0-1-1}.

Row 24: P 0{0-1-1}, K 0{0-1-9}, P2{6-10-10}, K 10, (P 10, K 10) across to last 2 sts, P2.

**Sizes Child, Small Adult, and Large Adult Only
Next {6-10-14} Rows:** Continue in pattern, moving spiral one stitch to the left every **right** side row by working one additional purl stitch following the knit edge stitch.

All Sizes: Cut Variegated.

CROWN SHAPING
Row 1: With Green, K6, P1, (K5, P1) across to last 1{5-5-1} st(s), K1{5-5-1}.

Row 2: P1{5-5-1}, K1, (P5, K1) across to last 6 sts, P6.

Row 3: K3, K2 tog, K1, P1, (K2, K2 tog, K1, P1) across to last 1{5-5-1} st(s), K1{2-2-1}, (K2 tog, K1) 0{1-1-0} time: 62{65-70-77} sts.

Row 4: P1{4-4-1}, K1, (P4, K1) across to last 5 sts, P5.

Row 5: K2, K2 tog, K1, P1, (K1, K2 tog, K1, P1) across to last 1{4-4-1} st(s), K1, (K2 tog, K1) 0{1-1-0} time: 50{52-56-62} sts.

Row 6: P1{3-3-1}, K1, (P3, K1) across to last 4 sts, P4.

Row 7: K1, K2 tog, K1, P1, (K2 tog, K1, P1) across to last 1{3-3-1} st(s), K1{0-0-1}, (K2 tog, K1) 0{1-1-0} time: 38{39-42-47} sts.

Row 8: P1{2-2-1}, K1, (P2, K1) across to last 3 sts, P3.

Row 9: K1, K2 tog across to last 1{2-1-2} st(s), K1{2-1-2}: 20{21-22-25} sts.

Row 10: P1, P2 tog across to last 1{2-1-2} st(s), P1{2-1-2}: 11{12-12-14} sts.

Cut yarn leaving a long end. Thread yarn needle with end and weave through remaining sts, gathering tightly to close. With same end, weave seam *(Fig. 9, page 34)*.

4-NEEDLE HAT

RIBBING

With Variegated and smaller size needles, cast on 72{76-80-88} sts and distribute evenly on double pointed needles; place marker *(see Markers, page 33)*, join to work in rounds, being careful not to twist.

Work in K2, P2 ribbing around for 1½" (4 cm), increasing 0{0-2-2} sts evenly spaced on last rnd *(see Zeros and Increasing Evenly Across a Row or Round, page 33)*: 72{76-82-90} sts.

BODY

Change to larger size needles.

Rnds 1 and 2: P 10, (K 10, P 10) around to last 2{6-12-0} sts, K2{6-10-0}, P 0{0-2-0}.

Rnds 3 and 4: K1, P 10, (K 10, P 10) around to last 1{5-11-19} st(s), K1{5-10-10}, P 0{0-1-9}.

Rnds 5 and 6: K2, P 10, (K 10, P 10) around to last 0{4-10-18} sts, K 0{4-10-10}, P 0{0-0-8}.

Rnds 7 and 8: K3, P 10, (K 10, P 10) around to last 19{3-9-17} sts, K 10{3-9-10}, P9{0-0-7}.

Rnds 9 and 10: K4, P 10, (K 10, P 10) around to last 18{2-8-16} sts, K 10{2-8-10}, P8{0-0-6}.

Rnds 11 and 12: K5, P 10, (K 10, P 10) around to last 17{1-7-15} st(s), K 10{1-7-10}, P7{0-0-5}.

Rnds 13 and 14: K6, P 10, (K 10, P 10) around to last 16{0-6-14} sts, K 10{0-6-10}, P6{0-0-4}.

Rnds 15 and 16: K7, P 10, (K 10, P 10) around to last 15{19-5-13} sts, K 10{10-5-10}, P5{9-0-3}.

Rnds 17 and 18: K8, P 10, (K 10, P 10) around to last 14{18-4-12} sts, K 10{10-4-10}, P4{8-0-2}.

Rnds 19 and 20: K9, P 10, (K 10, P 10) around to last 13{17-3-11} sts, K 10{10-3-10}, P3{7-0-1}.

Rnds 21 and 22: (K 10, P 10) around to last 12{16-2-10} sts, K 10{10-2-10}, P2{6-0-0}.

Rnds 23 and 24: P1, K 10, (P 10, K 10) around to last 1{5-11-19} st(s), P1{5-0-10}, K 0{0-1-9}.

Sizes Child, Small Adult, and Large Adult Only
Next {6-10-14} Rnds: Continue in pattern, moving spiral one stitch to the left, every two rounds, by beginning round with one additional purl stitch.

All Sizes: Cut Variegated.

CROWN SHAPING

Rnds 1 and 2: With Green, (K5, P1) around to last 0{4-4-0} sts, K 0{4-4-0}.

Rnd 3: (K2, K2 tog, K1, P1) around to last 0{4-4-0} sts, (K2, K2 tog) 0{1-1-0} time: 60[63-68-75] sts.

Rnd 4: (K4, P1) around to last 0{3-3-0} sts, K 0{3-3-0}.

Rnd 5: (K1, K2 tog, K1, P1) around to last 0{3-3-0} sts, (K1, K2 tog) 0{1-1-0} time: 48[50-54-60] sts.

Rnd 6: (K3, P1) around to last 0{2-2-0} sts, K 0{2-2-0}.

Rnd 7: (K2 tog, K1, P1) around to last 0{2-2-0} sts, K2 tog 0{1-1-0} time: 36{37-40-45} sts.

Rnd 8: (K2, P1) around to last 0{1-1-0} st, K 0{1-1-0}.

Rnd 9: (K2 tog, P1) around to last 0{1-1-0} st, K 0{1-1-0}: 24{25-27-30} sts.

Rnd 10: K2 tog around to last 0{1-1-0} st, K 0{1-1-0}: 12{13-14-15} sts.

Cut yarn. Thread yarn needle with end and weave through remaining sts, gathering tightly to close.

MITTENS

Work 2-Needle or 4-Needle Basic Mittens, pages 2-5, changing color in ribbing as follows *(see Changing Colors in Ribbing, page 33)*:

Cast on with Variegated and work 1¼{1½-1¾-1¾}" / 3{4-4.5-4.5} cm; change to Green and work ¾" (2 cm); then change to Variegated and work ½" (12 mm). Cut Variegated; with Green complete Mitten.

Instructions continued from page 10

Row 4: Purl across.

Row 5: K3{1-1-3}, K2 tog, (K2, K2 tog) across to last st, K1: 38{39-42-47} sts.

Row 6: Purl across.

Row 7: (K1, K2 tog) across to last 2{3-3-2} sts, K2{3-3-2}: 26{27-29-32} sts.

Row 8: Purl across.

Row 9: K1, K2 tog across to last 1{2-2-1} st(s), K1{2-2-1}: 14{15-16-17} sts.

Cut yarn leaving a long end. Thread yarn needle with end and weave through remaining sts, gathering tightly to close. With same end, weave seam *(Fig. 9, page 34)*.

4-NEEDLE HAT
RIBBING
With Yellow and smaller size needles, cast on 72{76-84-92} sts and distribute evenly on double pointed needles; place marker *(see Markers, page 33)*, join to work in rounds, being careful not to twist.

Work in K2, P2 ribbing around for 1½" (4 cm).

BODY
Change to larger size needles.

Rnd 1: (K3, slip 1) around.

Rnd 2: Knit around.

Repeat Rnds 1 and 2 for pattern until Hat measures approximately 3¼{3¾-4-4½}" / 8{9.5-10-11.5} cm from cast on edge, ending by working Rnd 1.

Next 4{4-6-6} Rnds: With Lt Blue, repeat Rnd 2 once, then repeat Rnds 1 and 2, 1{1-2-2} time(s); then repeat Rnd 1 once **more**.

Cut Lt Blue.

With Yellow, and beginning with Rnd 2, work in pattern until Hat measures approximately 5½{6½-7¼-8}" / 14{16.5-18.5-20.5} cm from cast on edge, ending by working a **knit** rnd.

CROWN SHAPING
Rnd 1: K4{2-4-6}, K2 tog, (K4, K2 tog) around: 60{63-70-77} sts.

Rnd 2: Knit around.

Rnd 3: K3{1-3-5}, K2 tog, (K3, K2 tog) across to last st, K1: 48{50-56-62} sts.

Rnd 4: Knit around.

Rnd 5: K2{0-2-4} *(see Zeros, page 33)*, K2 tog, (K2, K2 tog) around: 36{37-42-47} sts.

Rnd 6: Knit around.

Rnd 7: (K1, K2 tog) around to last 0{1-0-2} st(s), K 0{1-0-2}: 24{25-28-32} sts.

Rnd 8: Knit around.

Rnd 9: K2 tog around to last 0{1-0-0} st, K 0{1-0-0}: 12{13-14-16} sts.

Cut yarn. Thread yarn needle with end and weave through remaining sts, gathering tightly to close.

MITTENS
Work 2-Needle or 4-Needle Basic Mittens, pages 2-5, changing color in ribbing as follows:

Cast on with Yellow and work 3{4-4-4} rows/rnds; change to Lt Blue *(see Changing Colors in Ribbing, page 33)* and work 4{5-5-5} rows/rnds; change to Yellow and work 2 rows/rnds; change to Lt Blue and work 4{5-5-5} rows/rnds. Cut Lt Blue; with Yellow complete Ribbing to specified length.

Instructions continued from page 12

Row 4: Purl across.

Row 5: K3{1-1-3}, K2 tog, (K2, K2 tog) across to last st, K1: 38{39-42-47} sts.

Row 6: Purl across.

Row 7: (K1, K2 tog) across to last 2{3-3-2} sts, K2{3-3-2}: 26{27-29-32} sts.

Row 8: Purl across.

Row 9: K1, K2 tog across to last 1{2-2-1} st(s), K1{2-2-1}: 14{15-16-17} sts.

Cut yarn leaving a long end. Thread yarn needle with end and weave through remaining sts, gathering tightly to close. With same end, weave seam *(Fig. 9, page 34)*.

4-NEEDLE HAT
RIBBING

With White and smaller size needles, cast on 72{76-84-88} sts and distribute evenly on double pointed needles; place marker *(see Markers, page 33)*, join to work in rounds, being careful not to twist.

Rnds 1-4 (Right side): (K1, P3) around.

Rnd 5: With Tan, knit around *(see Changing Colors in Ribbing, page 33)*.

Rnd 6: Insert the left needle into the stitch **below** the next st on the left needle as if to **purl** and place it on the left needle, K2 tog, P3, (K1, P3) around.

Rnds 7 and 8: (K1, P3) around, increasing 0{2-0-2} sts evenly spaced on last rnd *(see Zeros and Increasing Evenly Across a Row or Round, page 33)*: 72{78-84-90} sts.

Cut Tan.

BODY
Change to larger size needles.

Rnd 1: With White, (K2, slip 1) around.

Rnd 2: Insert the left needle into the stitch **below** the next st on the left needle as if to **purl** and place it on the left needle, K2 tog, knit around.

Rnd 3: (K2, slip 1) around.

Rnd 4: Knit around.

Repeat Rnds 3 and 4 for pattern until Hat measures approximately 5½{6½-7¼-8}" / 14{16.5-18.5-20.5} cm from cast on edge, ending by working a **knit** rnd.

CROWN SHAPING
Rnd 1: (K4, K2 tog) around: 60{65-70-75} sts.

Rnd 2: Knit around.

Rnd 3: (K3, K2 tog) around: 48{52-56-60} sts.

Rnd 4: Knit around.

Rnd 5: (K2, K2 tog) around: 36{39-42-45} sts.

Rnd 6: Knit around.

Rnd 7: (K1, K2 tog) around: 24{26-28-30} sts.

Rnd 8: Knit around.

Rnd 9: K2 tog around: 12{13-14-15} sts.

Cut yarn. Thread yarn needle with end and weave through remaining sts, gathering tightly to close.

MITTENS
Work 2-Needle or 4-Needle Basic Mittens, pages 2-5, changing color in ribbing as follows *(see Changing Colors in Ribbing, page 33)*:

Cast on with White and work 7{7-9-9} rows/rnds; change to Tan and work 4{4-6-6} rows/rnds. Cut Tan; with White complete Ribbing to specified length.

General Instructions

ABBREVIATIONS

cm	centimeters
K	knit
mm	millimeters
M1	make one
M1P	make one purl
P	purl
Rnd(s)	Round(s)
st(s)	stitch(es)
tog	together

SYMBOLS & TERMS

★ — work instructions following ★ as many **more** times as indicated in addition to the first time.

( ) or [ ] — work enclosed instructions as **many** times as specified by the number immediately following **or** work all enclosed instructions in the stitch or space indicated **or** contains explanatory remarks.

colon (:) — the numbers given after a colon at the end of a row or round denote the number of stitches you should have on that row or round.

work even — work without increasing or decreasing in the established pattern.

GAUGE

Exact gauge is essential for proper fit. Before beginning your project, make a sample swatch in the yarn and needle specified in the individual instructions. After completing the swatch, measure it, counting your stitches and rows carefully. If your swatch is larger or smaller than specified, make another, changing needle size to get the correct gauge. Keep trying until you find the size needles that will give you the specified gauge.

KNIT TERMINOLOGY	
UNITED STATES	**INTERNATIONAL**
gauge =	tension
bind off =	cast off
yarn over (YO) =	yarn forward (yfwd) **or**
	yarn around needle (yrn)

Yarn Weight Symbol & Names	SUPER FINE 1	FINE 2	LIGHT 3	MEDIUM 4	BULKY 5	SUPER BULKY 6
Type of Yarns in Category	Sock, Fingering Baby	Sport, Baby	DK, Light Worsted	Worsted, Afghan, Aran	Chunky, Craft, Rug	Bulky, Roving
Knit Gauge Ranges in Stockinette St to 4" (10 cm)	27-32 sts	23-26 sts	21-24 sts	16-20 sts	12-15 sts	6-11 sts
Advised Needle Size Range	1-3	3-5	5-7	7-9	9-11	11 and larger

KNITTING NEEDLES															
U.S.	0	1	2	3	4	5	6	7	8	9	10	10½	11	13	15	17
U.K.	13	12	11	10	9	8	7	6	5	4	3	2	1	00	000	---
Metric - mm	2	2.25	2.75	3.25	3.5	3.75	4	4.5	5	5.5	6	6.5	8	9	10	12.75

▬□□□ BEGINNER		Projects for first-time knitters using basic knit and purl stitches. Minimal shaping.
▬▬□□ EASY		Projects using basic stitches, repetitive stitch patterns, simple color changes, and simple shaping and finishing.
▬▬▬□ INTERMEDIATE		Projects with a variety of stitches, such as basic cables and lace, simple intarsia, double-pointed needles and knitting in the round needle techniques, mid-level shaping and finishing.
▬▬▬▬ EXPERIENCED		Projects using advanced techniques and stitches, such as short rows, fair isle, more intricate intarsia, cables, lace patterns, and numerous color changes.

HINTS

As in all knitted pieces, good finishing techniques make a big difference in the quality of the piece. Do not tie knots. Always start a new ball at the beginning of a row, leaving ends long enough to weave in later. Make a habit of taking care of loose ends as you work. Thread a yarn needle with the yarn end. With **wrong** side facing, weave the needle through several stitches, then reverse the direction and weave it back through several stitches. When the ends are secure, clip them off close to the work.

MARKERS

Markers are used to help distinguish the beginning of each round being worked. Place a 2" (5 cm) scrap piece of yarn before the first stitch of each round, moving marker after each round is complete.

As a convenience to you, we have used markers to help distinguish the beginning of a pattern. Place markers as instructed. You may use purchased markers or tie a length of contrasting color yarn around the needle. When you reach a marker on each row or round, slip it from the left needle to the right needle; remove it when no longer needed.

ZEROS

To consolidate the length of an involved pattern, Zeros are sometimes used so that all sizes can be combined. For example, work across to last 0{1-2} sts means the first size would do nothing, the second size would K1, and the largest size would K2.

CHANGING COLORS IN RIBBING

When changing colors in ribbing, **knit** every stitch on the row or round in the new color. This eliminates the purl bumps of the old color showing on the **right** side of the piece. The knit row does not affect the elasticity of the ribbing.

INCREASING EVENLY ACROSS A ROW OR ROUND

Add one to the number of increases required and divide that number into the number of stitches on the needle. Subtract one from the result and the new number is the approximate number of stitches to be worked between each increase. Adjust the number as needed.

KNIT 2 TOGETHER
(abbreviated K2 tog)

Insert the right needle into the front of the first two stitches on the left needle as if to **knit** *(Fig. 1)*, then knit them together as if they were one stitch.

Fig. 1

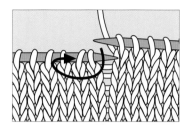

KNIT 3 TOGETHER
(abbreviated K3 tog)

Insert the right needle into the front of the first three stitches on the left needle as if to **knit** *(Fig. 2)*, then knit them together as if they were one stitch.

Fig. 2

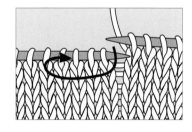

PURL 2 TOGETHER
(abbreviated P2 tog)

Insert the right needle into the front of the first two stitches on the left needle as if to **purl** *(Fig. 3)*, then purl them together as if they were one stitch.

Fig. 3

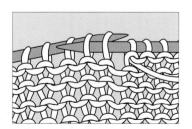

PURL 3 TOGETHER
(abbreviated P3 tog)

Insert the right needle into the front of the first three stitches on the left needle as if to **purl** *(Fig. 4)*, then purl them together.

Fig. 4

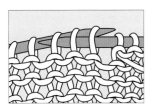

ADDING NEW STITCHES

Insert the right needle into stitch as if to **knit**, yarn over and pull loop through *(Fig. 5a)*, insert the left needle into the loop just worked from **front** to **back** and slip the loop onto the left needle *(Fig. 5b)*. Repeat for required number of stitches.

Fig. 5a   Fig. 5b

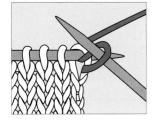 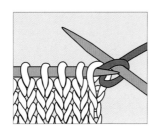

MAKE ONE *(abbreviated M1)*

Insert the left needle under the horizontal strand between the stitches from the **front** *(Fig. 6a)*. Then knit into the **back** of the strand *(Fig. 6b)*.

Fig. 6a   Fig. 6b

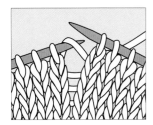 

MAKE ONE PURL *(abbreviated M1P)*

Insert the left needle under the horizontal strand between the stitches from the **back** *(Fig. 7a)*. Then purl into the **front** of the strand *(Fig. 7b)*.

Fig. 7a   Fig. 7b

PICKING UP STITCHES

When instructed to pick up stitches, insert the needle from the **front** to the **back** under two strands at the edge of the worked piece. Put the yarn around the needle as if to **knit** *(Fig. 8)*, then bring the needle with the yarn back through the stitch to the right side, resulting in a stitch on the needle.
Repeat this along the edge, picking up the required number of stitches.
A crochet hook may be helpful to pull yarn through.

Fig. 8

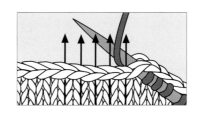

WEAVING SEAMS

With the **right** side of both edges facing you and edges even, sew through both sides once to secure the seam. Insert the needle under the bar between the first and second stitches on the row and pull the yarn through *(Fig. 9)*. Insert the needle under the next bar on the second side. Repeat from side to side, being careful to match rows.

Fig. 9

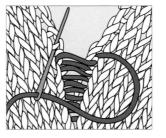

Yarn Information

The items in this leaflet were made using medium weight yarn. Any brand of medium weight yarn may be used. It is best to refer to the yardage/meters when determining how many balls or skeins to purchase. Remember, to achieve the same look, it is the weight of yarn that is important, not the brand of yarn.

For your convenience, listed below are suggested yarns to use.

Perfectly Pink Mittens
Red Heart® Super Saver®
#724 Baby Pink
#372 Rose Pink

Winter in the Tropics Set
Red Heart® Super Saver®
#994 Banana Berry Print

Winter Sunshine Set
Red Heart® Super Saver®
#324 Bright Yellow
#381 Lt Blue

Snow Drift Set
Red Heart® Super Saver®
#311 White
#330 Linen

Red Berries Set
Red Heart® Super Saver®
#319 Cherry Red
#886 Blue

Blue Ice Set
Red Heart® Super Saver®
#381 Lt Blue
#380 Windsor

Red Raspberry Set
Red Heart® Super Saver®
#930 Lipstick

Evergreen Set
Red Heart® Classic®
#957 Shaded Greens
#686 Paddy Green

We have made every effort to ensure that these instructions are accurate and complete.
We cannot, however, be responsible for human error, typographical mistakes,
or variations in individual work.

PRODUCTION TEAM:
Technical Writer/Editors: Joan Beebe, Jean Guirguis, and Peggy Greig
Editorial Writer: Susan McManus Johnson
Senior Graphic Artist: Lora Puls
Graphic Artist: Dave Pope
Photography Manager: Katherine Laughlin
Photostylists: Brooke Duszota and Sondra Daniel
Photographers: Larry Pennington and Ken West